CW00551842

NOTTINGHAMSHIRE & DERBYSHIRE TRAMWAY

Barry M Marsden

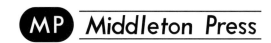

MP Middleton Press

Front cover: Two vehicles pause side-by-side on the turnout with Smedley's Hydro behind. They appear in their new 1898 livery after the undertaking was gifted to the UDC whose title can be seen on the cant rail. The trams appear in pristine condition, with the only adverts carried on the dash panels. Note the smart uniforms of the crews, which include kepi-style caps.

Back cover: A fine shot of an immaculate Car 17 on an early service run, posing in Heanor Market Place in 1913 on its way to Kimberley. Both crewmen parade in smart new uniforms. Note the conductor's white-topped summer cap, and the lengthy ladder on the left giving access to the bracket arm of the tram pole.

Cover colours: These represent the livery used by the Notts & Derby (light green and cream).

Published March 2005

ISBN 1 904474 53 5

© Middleton Press, 2005

Design Deborah Esher

Published by
> *Middleton Press*
> *Easebourne Lane*
> *Midhurst, West Sussex*
> *GU29 9AZ*
Tel: 01730 813169
Fax: 01730 812601
Email: info@middletonpress.co.uk
www.middletonpress.co.uk

Printed & bound by Biddles Ltd, Kings Lynn

The Nottinghamshire & Derbyshire Tramway 1 - 80
The Matlock Cable Tramway 81 - 120

CONTENTS
PART 1 - THE NOTTINGHAMSHIRE & DERBYSHIRE TRAMWAY

CONTENTS
PART 2 - THE MATLOCK CABLE TRAMWAY

INTRODUCTION AND ACKNOWLEDGEMENTS

The Nottinghamshire & Derbyshire Tramway was one of the last tramways to be constructed in Britain, and was conceived as an interurban network linking a series of towns and colliery villages in south-east Derbyshire and north-west Nottinghamshire, operating between Ripley and the City of Nottingham. Completed in 1913-14, it was 15 miles/24.1km long, and as such this stretch of single-line and loop trackway was the lengthiest in the British Isles, deploying 24 trams. It served a busy and growing population, but unfortunately the onset of World War I caused problems which it was never really able to overcome. After a post-war struggle with the competing motorbus, the undertaking re-equipped with trolleybuses in 1932, which themselves provided an exemplary service until their withdrawal in 1953.

Most of the photographs of the NDTC in this work come from the archives of the Crich Tramway Museum, though a significant number were kindly provided by the Heanor and District Local History Society, and the Nuthall and District Local History Society. To both societies I must express my deep gratitude, both for the images and for a number of identifications of the more obscure localities. I am also indebted to Glynn Waite for pictures of NDTC tickets from his own collection.

GEOGRAPHICAL SETTING

The route of the NDTC tramway crossed a part rural, part industrial landscape which included some of the Nottinghamshire and Derbyshire Coalfield, whose colliers provided much of the custom for the undertaking. As D.H. Lawrence pointed out in *Tickets, Please,* a short story in his book *England, My England,* the line climbed and fell as it passed through an undulating countryside, crossing canals and railway bridges as it traversed a series of towns and villages, with *'reckless swoops'* and *'breathless slithering'* round precipitous drops. Lawrence treated the journey as a great adventure, which it most probably was. Sadly, today, the route is much altered, with wholesale building obscuring the once open fields. Indeed, one of the once rustic villages, Nuthall, has since been severed by the M1 motorway!

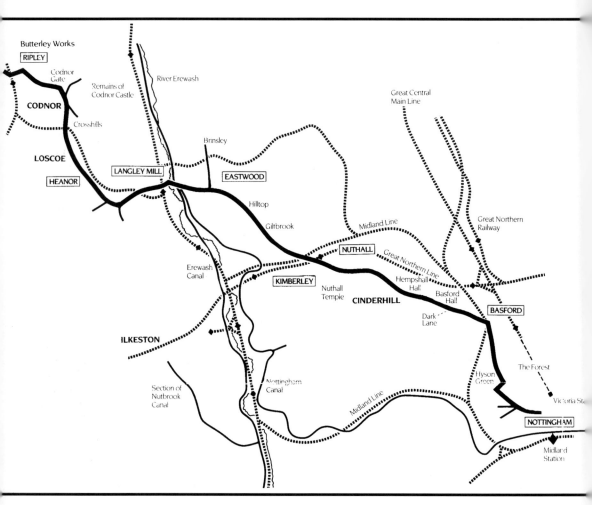

1.   The plan of the NDTC route shows that the 15 mile line ran from north-west to south-east, commencing at Ripley in Derbyshire and ending in the centre of Nottingham. Approximately one-third of the system ran through Derbyshire, and the car shed and offices were at Langley Mill.

HISTORICAL BACKGROUND

Once described by D.H. Lawrence as *'the most dangerous tram service in England',* the *'Ripley Rattlers'* - the green and cream tramcars of the Nottinghamshire & Derbyshire Tramways Company (NDTC) – were a familiar sight – and sound – to the inhabitants of the border towns and villages of South-East Derbyshire and North-West Nottinghamshire for some 20 years as they rumbled and swayed along the 15 miles of single track which linked the two urban termini of Ripley and Nottingham. Their route was the longest stretch of tramline in the British Isles and the full one-and-three-quarter hour journey from the shadow of the Ripley Co-operative Society to Nottingham Co-operative Society's headquarters on Upper Parliament Street must have required some passenger stoicism, riding on the hard wooden seats of the 13 ton 'Rattlers.'

When completed, the line was but the emasculated remnant of a network that was originally envisaged in 1903 as a vast 95 mile/ 153km system, with no less than five tramsheds and 316 passing loops, linking a wide area of villages and townships in East Derbyshire and West Nottinghamshire. However, fierce opposition, particularly from the Midland Railway, shaved down the proposed mileage, first to 79 miles, then 47, and finally a relatively puny 15, which included running powers over the Nottingham City metals, and a length of double track laid for it by the same undertaking from Cinderhill to Basford. It took ten years before the line, first promulgated in the Nottinghamshire and Derbyshire Tramways Act of 1903, became a reality, even in part, and it was one of the last tramways to be constructed in Britain.

The firm of Balfour, Beatty & Co. Ltd, formed in 1909, eventually purchased the company shares and, alert to the possibilities of the development of passenger transport and electricity supplies in the Midlands, formed, in 1912, the 'Midland Electric Light and Power Company' which also owned the Mansfield and Llanelly Tramways. They also possessed two local electricity supply undertakings, as well as the still unconstructed Notts & Derby enterprise, which they now determined to complete. The new line, built to standard gauge and 11.3 miles/18.1km in length, would pass through two counties, and no less than

five urban districts. One-third of its journey ran through Derbyshire, from Ripley, Codnor, Loscoe, Heanor and Langley Mill, where the tram depot was erected, then across the border into Eastwood, Kimberley, Nuthall and on to Cinderhill, where the track laid by Nottingham Corporation would take the route some 1.3 miles/2km further on, as far as the city's tramway terminus at Basford. From there the NDTCs cars would run the last 2.3 miles/3.7km into the heart of the county capital.

Construction of the line and overhead began at several points along the route in February 1913. Much time and labour was expended in the extensive programme of road widening necessary to push through the single-line and-loop tramtrack, which involved the wholesale demolition of walls and gardens and the realignment of frontages, together with the strengthening and broadening of several bridges along the route. The road below the railway bridge at Kimberley had to be lowered to facilitate the passage of the trams, whilst one at Eastwood had to be demolished and rebuilt to carry vehicles over the Nottingham and Erewash canals. At Heanor the 'White Horse' hostelry had to be pulled down, whilst the nearby 'Crown' was half-dismantled, but was kept open to retain its license. Local wags thereupon re-christened it the 'Half-Crown'!

Some 1000 labourers were employed in the construction of the line, providing much needed work in the locality. 1,500 tons of rail were used, and 20,000 tons of earth were removed to lay them. 10,000 tons of cement were needed, plus 12,000 tons of granite setts. Passing loops were positioned some 300 yds apart, all placed on the right-hand side of the track as it ran from Ripley to Nottingham, to allow city-bound cars the right of way. There were no less than 48 of these turnouts laid on the Company part of the line. The rails weighed 90lbs per yard, and the loops were fitted with spring-loaded points activated by the tram wheels. At the four railway crossings special rails of manganese toughened cast steel were supplied by the Titan Trackwork Company of Sheffield.

The motive power was provided by the old Derbyshire and Nottinghamshire Power Company generating station at Ilkeston, which had supplied current to Ilkeston Tramways since 1903. The Langley Mill depot, situated just within

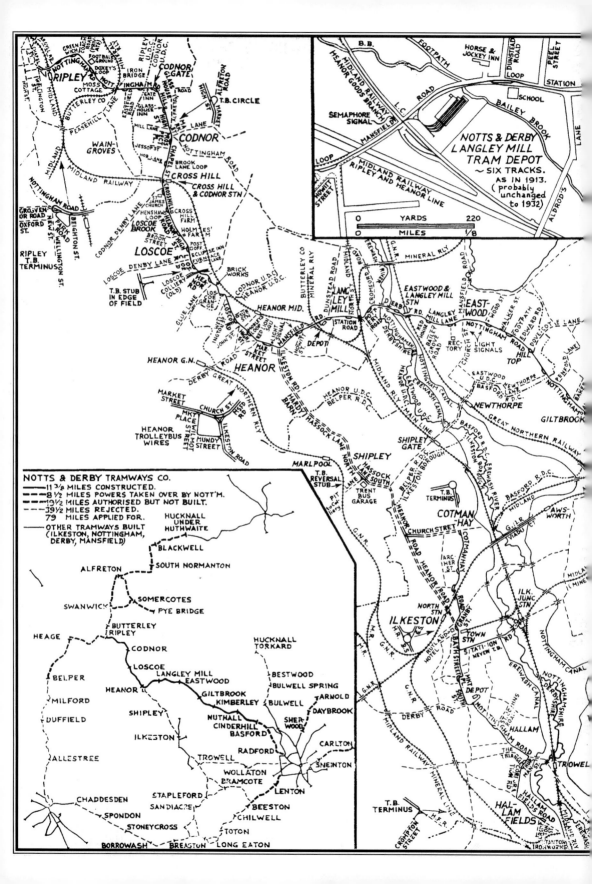

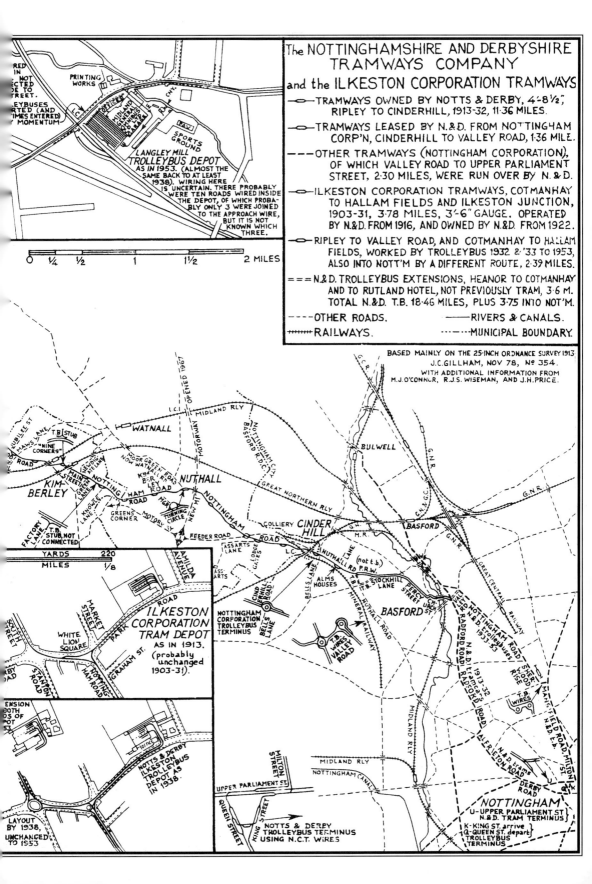

The NOTTINGHAMSHIRE AND DERBYSHIRE TRAMWAYS COMPANY
and the ILKESTON CORPORATION TRAMWAYS

- ⊷ TRAMWAYS OWNED BY NOTTS & DERBY, 4'-8½", RIPLEY TO CINDERHILL, 1913-32, 11·36 MILES.
- ⊷ TRAMWAYS LEASED BY N.& D. FROM NOTTINGHAM CORP'N, CINDERHILL TO VALLEY ROAD, 1·36 MILE.
- --- OTHER TRAMWAYS (NOTTINGHAM CORPORATION), OF WHICH VALLEY ROAD TO UPPER PARLIAMENT STREET, 2·30 MILES, WERE RUN OVER BY N. & D.
- ⊷ ILKESTON CORPORATION TRAMWAYS, COTMANHAY TO HALLAM FIELDS AND ILKESTON JUNCTION, 1903-31, 3·78 MILES, 3'-6" GAUGE. OPERATED BY N.& D. FROM 1916, AND OWNED BY N.& D. FROM 1922.
- ⊷ RIPLEY TO VALLEY ROAD, AND COTMANHAY TO HALLAM FIELDS, WORKED BY TROLLEYBUS 1932 & '33 TO 1953, ALSO INTO NOTT'M BY A DIFFERENT ROUTE, 2·39 MILES.
- === N.& D. TROLLEYBUS EXTENSIONS, HEANOR TO COTMANHAY AND TO RUTLAND HOTEL, NOT PREVIOUSLY TRAM, 3·6 M. TOTAL N.& D. T.B. 18·46 MILES, PLUS 3·75 INTO NOT'M.
- ---- OTHER ROADS.　　　——— RIVERS & CANALS.
- ++++++ RAILWAYS.　　　·—·—· MUNICIPAL BOUNDARY.

BASED MAINLY ON THE 25-INCH ORDNANCE SURVEY 1913
J.C.GILLHAM, NOV 78, No 354.
WITH ADDITIONAL INFORMATION FROM
M.J.O'CONNOR, R.J.S.WISEMAN, AND J.H.PRICE.

PRINTING WORKS

LANGLEY MILL TROLLEYBUS DEPOT
AS IN 1953. (ALMOST THE SAME BACK TO AT LEAST 1938). WIRING HERE IS UNCERTAIN. THERE PROBABLY WERE TEN ROADS WIRED INSIDE THE DEPOT, OF WHICH PROBABLY ONLY 3 WERE JOINED TO THE APPROACH WIRE, BUT IT IS NOT KNOWN WHICH THREE.

SPORTS GROUND

0　¼　½　1　1½　2 MILES

YARDS　220
MILES　1/8

ILKESTON CORPORATION TRAM DEPOT
AS IN 1913. (probably unchanged 1903-31).

WHITE LION SQUARE

NOTTS & DERBY ILKESTON TROLLEYBUS DEPOT AS IN 1938.

LAYOUT BY 1938, UNCHANGED TO 1953

WATNALL

KIMBERLEY

NUTHALL

BULWELL

CINDER HILL

BASFORD

NOTTINGHAM CORPORATION TROLLEYBUS TERMINUS

T.B. WIRES VALLEY ROAD

MILTON STREET

MIDLAND RLY
NOTTINGHAM CANAL

UPPER PARLIAMENT ST

QUEEN STREET
KING STREET

NOTTS & DERBY TROLLEYBUS TERMINUS USING N.C.T. WIRES

NOTTINGHAM
U - UPPER PARLIAMENT ST N.& D. TRAM TERMINUS
K - KING ST. arrive
Q - QUEEN ST. depart } TROLLEYBUS TERMINUS

the Derbyshire border, was served by six tracks, each intended to hold four fleet cars. The six lines narrowed down to two as the vehicles approached the road, just half a mile on the Derbyshire side of the border, where a 'Y' junction allowed the trams to turn either right or left along the main tramline.

Twenty-four trams were ordered by the company. Cars 1-12 were open-toppers, whilst 13-24 were balcony trams, all built by the United Electric Car Company (UECC) of Preston, and delivered in 'struck-down' condition, being assembled at the depot itself. The bodies were mounted on the reliable Peckham P22 pendulum trucks, built under licence by the Brush Company of Loughborough, and which were to receive a thorough testing out in the years that followed. The trams were powered by BTH GE203N 40hp motors and had the usual seating arrangements for the 56 passengers, 24 of whom travelled in the lower saloon on longitudinal wooden benches, and 32 on the top deck in a two-and-one arrangement of slatted swing-back garden seats. Interestingly enough the rolling stock carried no coats-of-arms or lettering on the lower side panels, only the fleet number in gold on each dash. The original motormen were drafted in from other Balfour Beatty enterprises, whilst the conductors appear to have been recruited locally.

Local commercial photographers were swift to retail postcards of the first trams to inaugurate the earliest services, after the usual trials, and it is not easy to work out which stretches of the line opened first. Indeed certain reports mention the commencement of different sections of the route over a period of some six months. One writer gives the date of July 4th for the initial Loscoe-Kimberley run, but a contemporary postcard shows Car 3 at Heanor, between these two points, with the legend 'HEANOR'S FIRST TRAMCAR JULY 29TH 1913'. This is backed up by the Heanor Observer which stated that the earliest service was the Crosshills-Cinderhill one, which began running on that date after an inspection by Lt-Col Druit of the Board of Trade (BoT). Two bridges along the route caused some early problems; at Crosshills serious structural defects to the fabric, probably caused by mining subsidence, forced the Company to foot the repair bill alone, whilst at Kimberley, where the roadway had already been lowered to allow the trams to pass beneath, the first balcony car to attempt passage, No.13, jammed itself firmly underneath the structure and had to be rammed

clear by an open-topper from behind. The road was then lowered for a second time.

Another postcard shows that Balcony Car 18 reached Eastwood, D.H. Lawrence's birthplace, on August 4th, and that the route was opened as far as Cinderhill by the 7th of the month after an inspection, again by Druit of the BoT. The Colonel also checked over the stretch between Crosshills and Ripley on the 15th, and the whole of the Company's line was then proclaimed fit for operations. Two further postcards show that Balcony Car 22 was the first to open the Ripley service. By the end of the year the Nottingham Corporation's line, from Cinderhill to Basford, was linked to the NDTC system, and was inspected by Major Pringle of the BoT on January 15th 1914. Trams were given permission for immediate running, and the whole of the 15 mile line was declared open.

Fares on the tramway were set at a penny a mile, with reductions if riders travelled over a number of sections. Five consecutive stages cost 4d, seven 6d, eight 7d, ten 8d eleven 9d and twelve 10d. An 11d ticket ensured a ride from Ripley to Basford, and the full journey cost an extra halfpenny. The usual workmens' fares were issued at half the price of ordinary ones, whilst colliers could travel as far as they wished for a flat 1d fee. Not many passengers travelled the whole length of the line; most rode on short journeys of three to four miles, resulting in frequent changes of travellers, who overlapped from stage to stage.

The timetable showed a half-hour frequency over most of the day, with the last car from Nottingham leaving at 11pm. This was, in crew parlance a 'flier', with unofficial limited stops and a fairly swift passage. Initial passenger returns were favourable, showing that during the first three months of the full service, some 19,000 route miles were run, transporting some 125,000 travellers.

In 1916 the company had purchased the ailing Ilkeston tramway with the eventual hope of connecting it to their own line at Heanor. In 1922 Parliamentary assent was granted to enable the NDTC to construct the tramway, but the junction of the two enterprises was not to be. Soon after the granting of assent the NDTC began developing a motorbus venture, the Midland General, with its promise of faster, more flexible and comfortable services over more direct routes. The buses actually ran in conjunction, and often in competition with the trams, and the Ilkeston – NDTC union did not become a reality until the trolleybus era.

In early 1922 the Company ordered three top covers from the English Electric Company of Preston. These were duly fitted to Cars 1-3 at the Langley Mill depot. Whether these were intended to be the first in a programme of upgrading the open-top fleet cars is not known, but no more trams were ever converted. Around this time the new manager decided that the Rattlers were too noisy, and ordered that the axleboxes be stuffed with sawdust. This was effective for a few weeks, until the ground-down material burst into spontaneous combustion, and the experiment was summarily abandoned!

By mid 1925 the tramway was reportedly losing some £30 per week, a factor not unconnected with rising unemployment in the district, particularly among colliery workers. In partial compensation the fare between Cinderhill and the city was cut from 3½d to 2d, and service frequencies were reduced. That same year the Company arranged to loan three of their open-top fleet vehicles to their sister undertaking at nearby Mansfield, for six months from July 1st at a rent of £200. They were towed to the town by a local fairground proprietor, though one had to be sent back to Langley Mill soon after, at the urgent request of the manager. In 1929 a Mansfield car was wrecked in a head-on collision with a motor bus, and the NDTC loaned them a balcony car to fill the gap.

Another rising problem was the proliferation of new motorbus services along the route, which offered swifter and more comfortable travel than the ageing, creaking NDTC rolling stock. An appeal to Parliament against this new menace under the terms of the 1903 Bill brought no relief, only a restriction on competition from new bus companies. By 1928 the Company had decided to replace the tramcars with trolleybuses, and re-christened themselves the Nottinghamshire and Derbyshire Traction Company in anticipation of this event.

In an effort to spruce up the decrepit tram fleet the Company embarked on a short-lived programme to renovate some of their conveyances. They first chose open-top Car 11, which had its lower saloon longitudinal benches ripped out and replaced with brown leather upholstered two-and-one transverse seating. The vehicle was freshly repainted in an unlined green livery, and had its equipment fully overhauled to eliminate hard-riding and transmission noise, though its upper deck remained unchanged. A

short time later Cars 9 and 12 joined the revamped rolling stock, and passengers rejoiced at the thoughts of a wholly refurbished system. However, although two further trams appeared in newly-painted condition, their interiors remained starkly utilitarian and the chances of pampered riding in the comfort of the remodelled lower saloons remained a lottery.

There are unconfirmed reports that, by 1930, twelve cars had been scrapped due to their poor condition, in addition to those loaned to Mansfield. By this time the Company had absorbed their omnibus rivals into their ranks, and had thus regained their former strong position in local transport. Fares on the tramway had shrunk in the meantime. Ripley to Cinderhill was now down to a shilling (adult return), and charges were only 50% of the corresponding bus fares. Revenues however continued to shrink – the old annual Nottingham Goose Fair, once a sure source of increased traffic receipts, had been shifted from the city Market Place to the outskirts. In 1928 a single NDTC tram ferrying riders home from this event carried, according to its motorman, Alfred Gillot, no less than 138 passengers on his 56 seater!

Matters had been put in hand to abandon the network in favour of trolleybus traction, and in August the Heanor-Ripley section was opened to railless use, leaving the Heanor-Cinderhill stretch to follow. One press report credits Motorman George Horsley, the oldest surviving driver, with manning the last car from Nottingham to the Langley Mill depot on September 3rd 1932. However other reports suggest that a service from Cinderhill to Basford continued for three further weeks, before Corporation buses took over until the NDTCs railless service commenced.

Other researchers contend that a workmen's car plied the route morning and evening between Heanor and Cinderhill for some time, but all are agreed that the last tram made the ultimate journey on October 5th driven by Charles Walker of Eastwood, to test the overhead wiring for the trolleybuses the day before they commenced running. 32 of the trackless inaugurated the new service, which connected with the Ilkeston system at Heanor, and they ran for some 20 years, roughly the same period as the Rattlers themselves. The remaining cars were either dismantled, or the bodies sold off locally. By this time the 31 year era of the electric tramcar was all but over in Derbyshire, with only sections of the Derby network still remaining operational.

Part 1 - THE NDT
RIPLEY

3.   The NDTC ordered 24 tramcars - Cars 13-24 being balcony versions such as this pristine example obviously photographed after assembly at Langley Mill. Note the lack of any logo apart from the company name in small letters at the base of the rocker panel. The shot includes a good view of the 7ft 6in/2286mm Peckham P22 trucks fitted to all the cars.

4. The iron railway bridge at Ripley is here shown undergoing strengthening in advance of the laying of the tramline. Several bridges along the route had to be either widened, raised by lowering the roadway underneath, or even rebuilt.

5.   By August 15th 1913 the NDTC line was running from Ripley as far as Cinderhill on the outskirts of Nottingham. This view shows the first tram into Ripley, Balcony Car 22, seen approaching the Co-operative building at top left, the Derbyshire terminus of the system, and welcomed by a sizeable throng of celebrating Ripleyites.

6.   Seen from the opposite side of the road, Car 22 shows off its lines at Ripley terminus, with the Co-op off to the right. The welcoming committee included deputy manager Stanley Dudman, sporting the boater, to the left, plus the chairman of Ripley Council, and the manager of the Co-op.

7.   I am always amazed at the size of the Ripley Co-operative Society building, feeling it far more befitting an edifice for a big city rather than a provincial town. Here, in this post-war view, an open-topper loads and unloads in the shadow of the building, whose fine turreted clock was a principal feature of the structure.

8.   Balcony Car 24 rests on the terminal loop in Co-operative Square, with the crew displaying some interest in the lifeguard. Note the primitive-looking jalopy on the right, and a possible relief tram crew posed on the left of the picture.

9.　　Taken from the opposite direction, Car 20, heading towards Ripley terminus, approaches along a narrow Nottingham Road. Hawkins' sweet shop, demolished in 1979, can be seen on the left.

10.　　Greenwich on the outskirts of Ripley, here seen looking west towards the town centre. Note the turnout in the foreground, encased in its bed of stone setts. All the loops were placed on the same side of the road to give cars heading for Nottingham the right of way, though this was often disputed by motormen travelling in the opposite direction!

CODNOR

11.   In this 1928 vista Car 16 heads towards Ripley along Nottingham Road, approaching the iron railway bridge near Steam Mill Lane on the left. The motorbus squeezing past on the right was operated by the rival firm of Williamsons.

12.   Open-topper Car 12 waits on the Nottingham Road loop at Codnor Gate, another 1920s shot judging by the attire of the young ladies on the right who might well have just disembarked from the conveyance. Sadly, the open fields on the left are now covered by the Codnor Gate Business Park.

13.   Another open-topper, well-loaded Car 6, pauses on the turnout at Codnor with the entrance to Prospect Place on the right. The motorman is still in 'civvies', suggesting an early date for the image. Note the metal stop sign on the bracket pole, which like all the posts in urban areas, bore wrought iron scrolling. On rural stretches of the line, they were left unadorned.

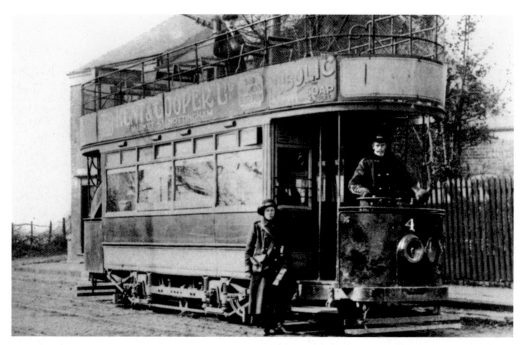

14.   A battered and war-weary Car 4 halts at Codnor in 1916 crewed by Motorman Martin and a Belgian refugee named Emla. Emla had a reputation for quelling troublesome riders with a blow from her ticket holder!

B 3329

The Nottinghamshire
and Derbyshire Tramways Co.

OUT		IN
Ripley	3d	Heanor Market
Codnor Gate		Langley Mill Ch.
Crosshill Church		Eastwood Market
Loscoe Crossing		Newthorpe Lane
Heanor Market		Digby Crossing
Langley Mill Ch.		James St. Kimberley
Eastwood Market		Nuttall Church
Hill Top		Lodge
Digby Crossing		Cinderhill

PUNCH & TICKET CO. LONDON. N1

LOSCOE

15.   An open-top car heads down Loscoe Hill towards Heanor in a sylvan locality populated only by the gent on the left with his wheelbarrow. Sheldon and Kirkman Roads lead off to the left; note the section box at the base of the left-hand bracket pole.

16.   Car 24 approaches the centre of Loscoe village along High Street, with Loscoe Denby Lane leading off to the left, and several horse-and-cart combinations in shot on this rural part of the route.

17.   A well-patronised Car 10 passes the Baptist Chapel in Loscoe on its way to Ripley during the first month of operations. Loscoe Denby Lane can be seen on the left, whilst the left-hand margins of the roadway reveal the tidying-up still necessary to restore the thoroughfare to its former state.

18.   Just south of the previous picture, earlier tracklaying along High Street is here shown in progress near Furnace Lane. The brand-new wall seen on the right was the frontage to Egreaves House, and can still be seen.

(top right) 19. Car 1, now top-covered in this post-1922 scene, grinds towards Heanor, with Loscoe Colliery just off shot to the left, behind the browsing horse. The sharp curve, north-west of Glue Lane, has now been ironed out, with part of it used as the entrance to a refuse amenity site.

The tramway manager placed this advert in the local press, giving details of the timetable in effect in 1914. It is interesting to note the appeal to visitors holidaying around Crich, in view of its later location as the National Tramway Museum. Incidentally, the 'nice walk' mentioned was some five miles long!

A Suggestion to Holiday Makers at Crich and District.

Spend an enjoyable day by having a Trip from

RIPLEY TO NOTTINGHAM
By ELECTRIC TRAMCAR.

Just a nice walk from Crich and a 15 miles run on the Car, passing through Codnor, Heanor, Langley Mill, Eastwood, Kimberley, Nuttall, and Cinderhill.

FARE: 11½d. EACH WAY.

CARS LEAVE —

RIPLEY FOR NOTTINGHAM:

WEEKDAYS.— 5.55, 6.35, 7.15, 7.45, 8.45 a.m., and every 30 minutes until 9.15 p.m.

SATURDAYS. As above, and every 30 minutes until 1.45 p.m., then every 15 minutes until 5.0 p.m., and every 12 minutes until 9.24 p.m.

SUNDAYS. 11.15 a.m. and every 15 minutes until 8.15 p.m.

NOTTINGHAM (Parliament Street) FOR RIPLEY:

WEEKDAYS.—7.30 a.m. and every 30 minutes until 8.0 p.m., then 8.45 p.m. (last thro' Car).

SATURDAYS. —7.30 a.m., and every 30 minutes until 12.0 noon, then every 15 minutes until 4.15 p.m., then 4.24 and every 12 minutes until 8.36 p.m., then 9.0, 9.15, and 10.0 p.m. (last thro' Car).

SUNDAYS.—10.15 a.m. and every 15 minutes until 8.0 p.m. (last thro' Car).

Nottinghamshire & Derbyshire Tramways Company,
LANGLEY MILL.

Tele. No. 53 Langley Mill.   C. R. WALKER, Manager.

20.   An open-topper approaches the Loscoe Grange turnout by the Sir John Warren pub on its way to Heanor. Despite the semi-rural nature of the locality the bracket poles are still adorned with their wrought iron scrolling.

21.   A close-up of the vehicle shows it to be Car 6, pausing opposite Loscoe Grange, the road seen on the extreme left. The stop sign on the pole is in front of the Sir John Warren Hotel. Note the Sunlight Soap advert in the field on the right.

22.   Car 13 at rest opposite the same inn, as it halts for a photograph. The tram is bound for Cinderhill, presumably before the opening of the full system. The motorman is Edward Stevens, and the trainee conductor Frank Llawes. Note the individual on the right with the laundry basket balanced on his head.

23.   Car 24 at rest on the High Street turnout near Milward Road by the old brickworks. The tram is only just within the Loscoe boundary, and the photographer probably set up his camera within the Heanor UDC boundary to take his picture!

L 6190

The Nottinghamshire
and Derbyshire Tramways Co.

OUT	2d	IN
Wood-linkin Road		Heanor Market
Heanor Market	This Ticket is available on day of issue only and not subject to Bye-laws. Must be retained for inspection, and given up on demand.	Midland Hotel Langley Mill
Langley Mill Church		East-wood Market
Nuttall Church		Cinder-hill

HEANOR

24.　　Judging that the crew of gleaming new Balcony Car 14 are dressed in mufti, this shot, taken on the Loscoe Road loop with Allandale Road just behind the tram on the left, would suggest a proving run before the opening of the service.

25.　　Car 1 climbs High Street on the approach to Red Lion Square on a summer day in 1913, with the upper deck seats well-stocked in the sunshine. Note the branch of Boot's Chemist on the right, which originated in Nottingham, and boasted that the organisation was 'the largest retail chemists in the world.'

26.   Car 21 descends Market Street on the way to Ripley in this World War 1 scene, with the squat tower of St Lawrence's Church visible in the distance. On the left is the Empire Cinema, which opened in 1911, and whose attractions that week included a topical film appropriately called 'The Curse of War.'

27.　　Car 21 again, possibly taken on the same day as picture 26 as it heads down Market Street. Ray Street leads off to the left with Redfern's corner shop displaying a variety of goods outside the premises.

28.　　A fine shot of an immaculate Car 17 on an early service run, posing in Heanor Market Place in 1913 on its way to Kimberley. Both crewmen parade in smart new uniforms. Note the conductor's white-topped summer cap, and the lengthy ladder on the left giving access to the bracket arm of the tram pole.

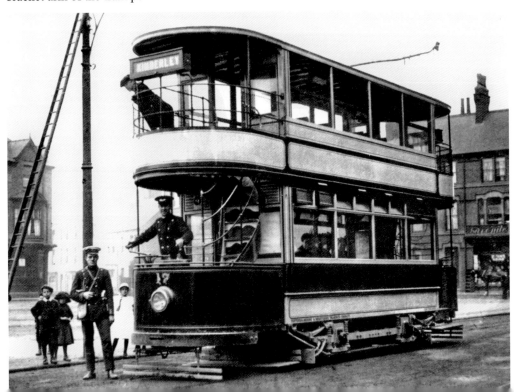

29.   Another picture of Car 17 in the Market Place, this time on passage to Ripley, probably after World War 1. The traction pole now holds a metal stop sign, and St. Lawrence's tower looms behind the vehicle. Note also the motorbus visible behind the passenger climbing aboard the tram.

30.   Another post-war view catches a balcony car picking up trade outside the Heanor Furnishing Stores as it pauses by the open-topped hot-rod visible on the left. Had the complete 1903 plans for the NDTC gone ahead, the Market Square would have become an important tramway interchange.

31.   Presumably an early practice run for Car 5 as it pauses on a blitzed-looking Church Street with the remains of the part-demolished Crown Inn behind. The white-capped figure is again Motorman Edward Stevens (see picture 22), who may have been instructing the other two drivers. The bearded ancient on the right looks suitably impressed by the advent of the new electric-powered traction.

32.   Captioned 'HEANOR'S FIRST TRAM JULY 29TH 1913' this view catches open-top Car
3 on Church Street, under the gaze of bemused spectators and crewed presumably by UECC
personnel. The house on the right is The Dene, at one time the home of the Quaker writer William
Howitt.

33. Car 3 pauses for its picture higher up Church Street, with The Dene visible at centre left. Piles of spoil on the right attest to the disruption caused by the widespread road widening necessitated by tracklaying operations.

S 1582

The Nottinghamshire
and Derbyshire Tramways Co.

OUT		IN
Ripley		Codnor Gate
Codnor Gate	1½D	Crossbill Church
Crossbill Church		Loscoe Crossing
Loscoe Crossing		Heanor Market
Heanor Market		Lang Mill G.
Mid. Hotel Langley M		Eastwood Market
Eastwood Market		Newthorpe Lane
Hill Top		Digby Crossing
Digby Crossing		James St.
ames St. Kimberley		Kimberley
		Nuttall Church
Nuttall Church		Lodge
Lodge		Cinderhill
Cinderhill		Church St. Basford

Available only on Car on which issued, subject to the Co.'s bye—laws & Regulation., Must be retained for Inspection or given up on demand.

PUNCH & TICKET CO. LONDON, N1

34.   Balcony Car 14 is here seen climbing Mansfield Road on the way to Heanor, passing well-built suburban villas on the right. The photograph was taken at the junction with Howitt Street on the right.

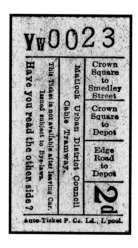

LANGLEY MILL

35.   Cars 1 and 2 were the first of the NDTC open-toppers, and were delivered to the depot in 'struck-down' condition, to be assembled there. In this scene they appear to be complete apart from the fitting of the trolleybooms. After World War 1 both these cars were top-covered.

36.   A view of the front of the car shed includes several of the open-toppers approaching completion. Car 12 appears on the left, with Car 11 to the right. The open bays of the depot can be clearly seen, with the rails curving out to join the single line leading out onto the main Mansfield Road to the left.

37.   This photograph, taken looking east along Mansfield Road, shows the entrance to the depot on the right. An open-topper and a balcony car can be seen in the depot yard, whilst in the foreground the track of the Heanor goods branch of the Midland Railway crosses the thoroughfare via a level crossing.

Bh **9135**

The Nottinghamshire
and Derbyshire Tramways Co

BETWEEN

Ripley	FARE	Codnor Gate
Codnor Gate	**1**d	Crosshill Church
Crosshill Church		Loscoe Crossing
Woodlinkin Road		Heanor Market
Heanor Market		Mid. Hotel Langley Mill
Langley Mill Church		Eastwood Market
Eastwood Market		Newthorpe Lane
Hill Top		Greasley Schools
Digby Cross Inn		James St. Kimberley
James St. Kimberley		Nuttall Church
Nuttall Church		Cinderhill
Cinderhill		Church Street

This Ticket is issued subject to the Company's Bye-laws and Regulations, and must be shown for Inspection or given up on demand.

38.   A close-up study of Balcony Car 14 was taken just outside the depot sometime during the early years of the facility. Note the driver's platform, which remained unvestibuled during the service life of all the trams.

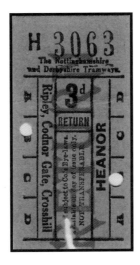

39. Langley Mill staff, including inspectors, motormen and conductors are arrayed in front of their vehicles in the tram shed, at the start of enterprise. The seated central figure was probably the manager, C.R. Walker. Note the curving lines of the tracks below the posing group of figures.

H 6320

The Nottinghamshire
and Derbyshire Tramways Co.

OUT	2d	IN
Ripley		Crosshill Church
Codnor Gate		Loscoe Crossing
Crosshill Church		Heanor Market
Loscoe Crossing		Langley Mill Ch.
Mid. Hotel Langley M		Newthorpe Lane
Eastwood Market		Digby Crossing
Hill Top		James Kimberley
Digby Crossing		Nuttall Church
James St. ...horley		Lodge

40.   Balcony Car 20, its destination box reading 'SPECIAL', appears on a pre-service test run near Dunstead Road, staffed presumably by UECC personnel. Note the parlous state of the road margins.

41.   Looking towards Heanor along Station Road, Langley Mill, reveals the squat tower of St Andrew's Church, completed in 1912, and a balcony car heading west into Derbyshire. The tram has stopped on the North Street loop to pick up passengers.

42.   Another, post-war, view of Station Road, showing the single line of the tramway. The memorial on the right bank was to local men who died in the Boer War. It will be seen that the bracket poles, which bore scrollwork in the previous picture, are now totally bare. Note the cabling on one of the posts, feeding power to the overhead.

⟶

43.   A good frontal study of Car 18 carefully posed on Station Road, Langley Mill, on a summer's day judging by the motorman's white-topped cap. The conductor has yet to receive his uniform issue, and the passenger posed on the upstairs balcony is very keen to get in shot.

44.　　An open-topper has come to grief in front of the Wesleyan Chapel in this post-war picture, with North Street just behind the bull-nosed Morris on the right. The usual crowd is in attendance, whilst one of the bystanders is determined to hide the fleet number of the vehicle.

45.　　A wartime image has Car 13 with its mixed crew on Station Road, at the foot of Dunstead Road. The tram is Nottingham bound, the conductress having neglected to turn the destination blind! Note the non-standard cap badges worn by the pair. The lady is sporting a Royal Artillery badge, whilst the crossed swords of the motorman are reminiscent of U.S. Cavalry emblems at the time of the Indian Wars!

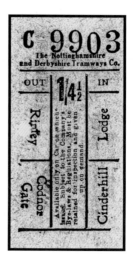

EASTWOOD

46.   Entitled 'EASTWOOD'S FIRST CAR AUG 4,' Balcony Car 18 is here seen pioneering the inaugural run to D.H. Lawrence's birthplace from the Langley Mill depot as indicated on the destination blind. The car, which is facing west on Nottingham Road, has attracted a fair selection of the locals. The gabled building at the top right is the Empire Cinema.

47.   Another view of the 13-ton vehicle shows 'DEPOT' as its destination as it poses behind a large congregation of Eastwoodites of all ages, including the young lady on the right, who is balancing on a single roller-skate.

48.   Further east along Nottingham Road Car 1 is pictured with its wholly 'civvy' crew, perhaps on an earlier incursion by the NDTC to the township.

NOTTINGHAM ROAD
EASTWOOD
REX SERIES

49.	Looking west along Nottingham Road, in this post-war vista, a distant open-topper approaches on the way to Nottingham. Note the baroque frontage of the Empire Cinema, opened in 1912, with King Street on the extreme right of the photograph.

50.	Another photo was taken along the same road, with the single line running down the centre of the thoroughfare. Note the host of blinds fronting the shops, whilst the nearest bracket pole still holds on to its wrought-iron scrolling, and also bears a metal stop sign.

51.	At Hill Top, on the eastern outskirts of Eastwood, a distant balcony car makes for Nottingham. Dovecoat Road leads off to the left, and in the foreground can be seen the points of the long passing loop laid here. Note the stove-enamelled stop sign on the traction pole on the left, which seems in need of a good clean.

KIMBERLEY

52.   A poor photograph, but it shows one of the NDTC balcony cars on Main Street, halted outside the Main Street Methodist Chapel. Note the horse trough sunk in the road at bottom right, which was fed by a local spring. Just off the picture to the right was the 'Coronation Oak,' planted to commemorate the crowning of King Edward VII.

53.   Main Street, Kimberley, looking west, with the Queen's Head Inn on the left, and the Great Northern Hotel just above the GNR bridge which once took the railway through the village. It was under this bridge that Balcony Car 13 became jammed in 1913. This post-war shot shows the overhead being carried on bracket poles not yet shorn of their adornment.

54.   A little further east open-top Car 6 waits at the stop on its way to Ripley. The Queen's Head can be seen on the left, below the receiving office of the Heanor Laundry Company.

NUTHALL

55. Moving east towards Nottingham, Balcony Car 24 runs alongside the eight-foot high wall bounding the Temple Estate, which ran as far west as the edges of Kimberley. Note the light painted bracket pole, and the passing loop in the foreground.

56. Along Kimberley Road in the 1920s, young Frank Mumby poses for his picture along an idyllic countryside part of the route. A stop sign can be seen on the near-distant pole, and the building on the left was known as The Cottage.

57. Looking east along Kimberley Road, the camera picks out a balcony tram approaching the turnout alongside Temple Lodge, just off shot on the left. The buildings include the Institute and Reading Room to the right of the car, and the Goat's Head pub which boasts the casement window.

58.   Taken from the opposite direction, Car 17, Ripley bound, halts on the loop, whilst a blurred open-topper hastens towards Nottingham, too fast for the camera to catch. The Institute stands on the left, and Temple Lodge on the right.

59.   Another view of Temple Lodge, with open-top tram No.2 halted on the loop in a snowy landscape. The motorman wears necessary oilskins and gauntlets, and many tales are told of hypothermic drivers freezing on their windswept, unvestibuled platforms. Though the destination is shown as Ripley, the trolleyboom has yet to be swung for the return, on what was presumably a short-working.

NOTTINGHAM

60.   Unfortunately, views of NDTC cars operating on the line beyond Nuthall, and through Cinderhill and Basford, are rare. This image shows Balcony Tram 22 approaching Canning Circus on a dismal, wet day, on its way into the city, operating over the tracks of Nottingham Corporation Tramways.

61.   Another top-covered car, No.18, approaches Canning Circus from the opposite direction, on a much better day, climbing up Derby Road on its way out of the city on its return to Ripley in this post-World War 1 scene.

NOTTINGHAM TERMINUS

62.   Car 1, which was later top-covered, waits at the terminus on Upper Parliament Street, its dash panel bearing a nasty scratch. Note the board in the side window, listing its destination and intermediate stops.

63.   A fine shot of Balcony Car 16, seen at the same venue in 1916, near another Co-operative building, in this case the local headquarters of Nottingham Co-op. By this time the 'Rattlers' had become liberally adorned with adverts.

64. On a rainy day in July 1930, open-top tram No.12 awaits trade in front of Nottingham Corporation Balcony Tram 196, with the Three Horseshoes Hotel forming a backdrop to the scene.

B 3329

The Nottinghamshire
and Derbyshire Tramways Co.

OUT		IN
Ripley	**3**d	Heanor Market
Codnor Gate		Langley Mill Ch.
Crosshill Church		Eastwood Market
Loscoe Crossing		Newthorpe Lane
Heanor Market		Digby Crossing
Langley Mill Ch.		James St. Kimberley
Eastwood Market		Nuttall Church
Hill Top		Lodge
Digby Crossing		Cinderhill

PUNCH & TICKET CO. LONDON.

CARS AND CREWS

Rolling Stock

Cars 1 - 12 Built by UEC in 1913 and equipped with Peckham P22 trucks. **Cars 1- 3** (Originally open top) of this series were fitted with balcony top covers in 1922. **Cars 13 - 24**. Top covered trams built by UEC and delivered in 1913. Seating for both batches of vehicles was given as 24 lower deck and 32 upper deck.

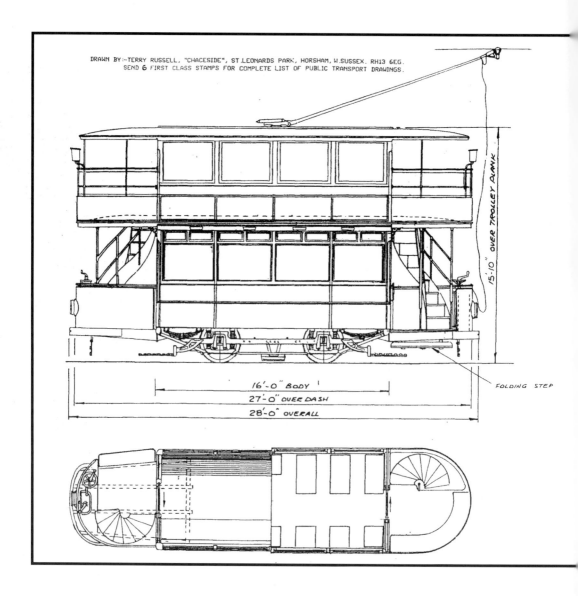

DRAWN BY:-TERRY RUSSELL, "CHACESIDE", ST.LEONARDS PARK, HORSHAM, W.SUSSEX. RH13 6EG. SEND 6 FIRST CLASS STAMPS FOR COMPLETE LIST OF PUBLIC TRANSPORT DRAWINGS.

15'-10" OVER TROLLEY PLANK

16'-0" BODY
27'-0" OVER DASH
28'-0" OVERALL

FOLDING STEP

65.   Many views of the NDTC trams and their crews were taken at various localities, some of which cannot now be identified. Here Car 4 is pictured with motorman, conductor and inspector, probably at Langley Mill.

(lower right) 66. A rather battered shot of Car 13, taken in summer judging by the white-topped cap and the foliage on the left. The motorman has been identified as Driver Large.

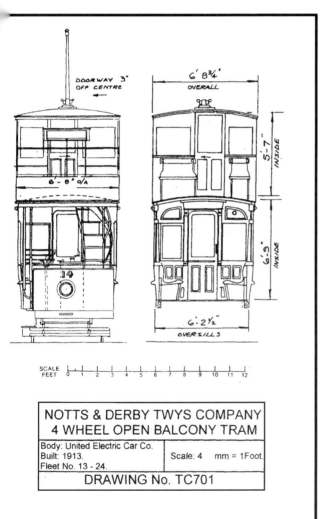

NOTTS & DERBY TWYS COMPANY
4 WHEEL OPEN BALCONY TRAM

Body: United Electric Car Co.	
Built: 1913.	Scale: 4 mm = 1Foot.
Fleet No. 13 - 24.	

DRAWING No. TC701

67.   Two Balcony trams, including Car 22 are here seen carrying a large party of youthful men and women in their best attire, bound on some sort of excursion, perhaps a Sunday School treat.

68.   A wartime scene was taken at Ripley as Car 1 waits to begin a short-working to Heanor. Note the grizzled veteran of a motorman and his smiling conductress, whilst the local youth have been roped in to give variety to the photograph.

69. A superb studio shot of Conductress Annie Bronson, who could well have been the model for D.H. Lawrence's Annie Stone. He wrote of the wartime female NDTC staff that *'The girls are fearless young hussies. In their ugly blue uniform, skirts up to their knees, shapeless old peaked caps on their heads, they have all the sang froid of an old non-commissioned officer.'*

70. An inspector, motorman and smiling conductress pose on and in front of a weathered open-top Car 2 in this illustration dating from the middle years of the First World War.

71.   At Langley Mill Car 16 and its crew pauses in this summer shot
for its photograph, with a family peering out from the upper-deck balcony,
obviously on their way for an outing.

LATTER DAYS

72.   Late in the history of the NDTC the company began a programme of revamping some of the rolling stock. Car 11 was the first to be updated, receiving an all-over bright green livery and transverse upholstered brown leather seating in the lower saloon. The renovated vehicle is here pictured at Ripley terminus, with the motorman modelling a rather fetching heavy-duty apron.

73.   Car 9 was the next to receive the treatment, and is shown here at the same venue. Note that the tram has lost its indicator boxes, whilst the tops of the transverse seat backs can just be seen in the lower compartment.

74.   The last of the three trams to be converted was Car 12, again photographed at Ripley. Unlike Car 9, this vehicle has retained its indicator boxes.

75.   A shot of the same car taken from the opposite direction. in watery sunshine on a damp day, probably at the same time as picture 74. The conductor is disembarking, presumably to swing the trolleyboom for the return trip

76.   Judging by this picture, taken of a balcony car with the Ripley Ebeneezer Chapel behind, some of the top-covered trams sported a revised livery in the last days of the facility. Note that apart from the narrow band under the top-deck windows, the car has been repainted in overall green.

77.   This picture, also taken at the Ripley terminus, may represent the same car after turning at the depot. The window bills seem positioned in the same places, and the paint scheme is identical.

78.   Several NDTC trams were loaned to the sister Mansfield undertaking in 1926, and this scene shows a re-numbered Car 30 in Stockwell Gate, next to the town's market, in 1932.

79.   In 1933 trolleybuses replaced trams on the Ripley-Nottingham run. Here one of the Weymann-bodied BUT9611T double-deckers, No.344 (NNU 225) passes St Patrick's Church, Nuthall on its way to Nottingham in the 1950s.

80.   On the last day of trolleybus operation, 25th April 1953, another BUT two-decker passes through Nuthall *en route* to Nottingham.

PART 2 – THE MATLOCK CABLE TRAMWAY

CONTENTS

INTRODUCTION AND ACKNOWLEDGEMENTS

The Matlock Cable Tramway was the first non-horse undertaking to be built in Derbyshire. The brain-child of Job Smith, a local businessman, it was financed by another Matlock native, Sir George Newnes, a successful publisher, who later presented it to Matlock Urban District Council as a gift. The tramway opened in 1893 with three Milnes-built open-top trams as rolling stock, and served both visitors and the local population for 34 years, until its demise in 1927, by which time it had become something of a white elephant. Nevertheless the tramway had several claims to fame and its history is a fascinating piece of tramway lore.

For photographs and information on the facility I am indebted to David Nutt, the Arkwright Society, the Derbyshire Library Service, Glynn Waite and the Science Museum to whom I offer my gratitude and appreciation.

GEOGRAPHICAL SETTING

The town of Matlock is set on a steep hillside above the River Derwent amid the picturesque limestone hills and dales of the Derbyshire Peak, and has been an inland resort and Spa for over 200 years. In the mid-19th century the Midland Railway was pushed through the valley, and a station was opened at Matlock Bridge in 1849, providing excellent access for tourists and visitors relaxing at the many spas which proliferated on the heights of the town in the latter part of the 1800s. When the cable tramway opened in 1893 it provided easy access up the steep hillside for votaries seeking both recreation and the water treatment available at the many hilltop establishments.

HISTORICAL BACKGROUND

The first hydro was opened in the town in 1853. Hydropathic establishments were becoming popular at the time, and a number of other competitors set up in business on the steep hillside of Matlock Bank. Matlock entered a boom period as customers flocked to try the newfangled treatment, and the arrival of the Midland Railway, linking the spa to London and Manchester, swiftly helped its expansion. The town rapidly attained the status of a widely patronised inland resort.

The idea for a tramway linking Crown Square at the foot of the hill with the top of Matlock Bank originated with Job Smith, a native of Matlock, who first saw the cable trams in San Fransisco. He suggested that a similar system up Matlock hill might prove a sound investment, linking the railway with the hillside spas, but the highest part of the route, Rutland Street, was too narrow for trams, and the idea languished. However by 1890 Smith had become a member of the local board, and as the offending street had by that time been widened, he mooted the project again. George Croydon Marks, engineer to the Lynton Cliff Railway, saw a report on the scheme, and discussed it with George Newnes MP, another Matlock native, and a noted publisher. Newnes offered to finance the undertaking, powers were granted, and work commenced on the depot. Originally this was to be erected near Matlock Bridge, but periodic flooding in this area led to an alternative site, at the top of the hill.

Marks became the company engineer and Dick, Kerr & Co. were contracted to lay the line. It was to be single track, 0.62 miles/1km long with one passing loop at Smedley Street, halfway up the slope. The enterprise became the first single-line cable tramway in Europe, and the maximum gradient – 1ft in 5.5ft – made it the steepest street tramway anywhere in the world. The track gauge was fixed at 3ft 6in/1067mm with a central slot rail beneath which ran a conduit holding the continuous 3in cable. This ran endlessly in its channel from the steam-powered engine room, round a tensioning mechanism and guide rails, down the hill, round further wheels in an underground chamber in Crown Square, and back up the hill again. The route contained some sharp curves, one of 40ft radius, which necessitated special pulleys to support and carry the cable round. The track climbed an elevation of 300ft in 2,300 to the upper terminus alongside the main depot.

The trial trip on 12th November 1892 was run at a speed of 6mph, with G.F. Milnes of Hadley supplying the three cars, all open-top double-deckers with transverse garden seats on both decks, providing places for 31 passengers. The vehicles were painted in royal blue and white, with numbers on the dash panels, and the company logo on the waist panel. They were mounted on equal four-wheel bogies, and had two braking systems, one an emergency one to the rail, powerful enough to stop the tram when free-running. To start the car the driver operated a 'gripper' mounted under the stairs at each end of the car body. This device passed through the narrow slot in the rail, and had a clamp at its base. By turning a screw via a handwheel the driver could lock the soft metal jaws of the gripper to the continuous-moving cable. To stop the tram he released the cable by opening the jaws and applying the brake. Both brakes were workable from either platform, by the driver or conductor.

The tramway was inspected on 7th March 1893 by Major General Hutchinson, who fixed the cable speed at 5.5mph. There was a turnout in Crown Square, and at the depot a sharp left turn led the cars into a yard where all three vehicles could stand on the level. A traverser led to three short tracks within the shed, each holding one tram. The service was normally run by two cars, which counterbalanced each other, with a third on standby. The last car up the hill at night, always fully loaded, caused problems as it struggled up the slope at a snail's pace! The depot, which boasted a 100ft tall chimney together with a waiting room and 'other conveniences', cost £2,600.

The line opened on 28th March 1893 with great pomp and ceremony. The town was *en fete* for the occasion with flags and banners and floral arches. A host of dignitaries accompanied the procession, and a banquet at the Assembly Rooms was attended by 120 guests. Food and wine flowed freely, and laudatory speeches heralded the newly installed facility.

In its first year the system was a great success, transporting over 250,000 riders during the high season, and earning profits of £204, whilst a 2% dividend was declared on the £15,000 share capital. It was, alas, the only one ever enjoyed by the shareholders. Cables only lasted an average of two years, perhaps due to the wear caused by the short radius curves. After five years, Newnes, by now a knight, bought out his fellow shareholders and presented the tramway as a gift to the town. On 28th June 1898 it was handed over to Matlock UDC, with a formal ceremony following on 26th October. The council became the first municipal authority to own a cable tramway, and the only one to acquire one as a gift! By this time it was understood that the undertaking was more of an amenity than a profit-making concern, though for many years losses were fairly small.

In 1899 a picturesque tram shelter was built in Crown Square, surmounted by a fine four-faced public clock topped by ornamental iron scrollwork, all donated by local businessman Robert Wildgoose. The ornate little edifice appears on many photographs taken during the life of the tramway, and was afterwards dismantled and rebuilt in a nearby park. When the council took over the cable cars, the legend MATLOCK URBAN DISTRICT COUNCIL TRAMWAY appeared on the cant rail above the tram windows. Gradually advertisements were added, many of them related to the plethora of hydropathic establishments flourishing along the bank.

After municipalization the trams continued their valuable service, and in 1911 a fourth vehicle was added to the fleet, a locally-built single-decker adapted from a double-deck Birmingham cable car. Unfortunately the vehicle was provided with longitudinal seating, and riders found themselves sliding to the bottom end of the tram as it moved up and down the hill. The car was sold off in 1916, and is so far photographically almost non existent.

Up to 1913 losses on the undertaking were acceptable, but from 1917 the financial position deteriorated rapidly, and the UDC faced deficits of around £1000 a year, one of the problems being increasing maintenance costs. In 1920 the expensive steam engines were replaced by a gas plant, but winter losses continued to escalate, despite the uprating of fares. A rival motorbus service, calling at both termini via a circuitous route, added further pressure to the ailing cableway.

In July 1927 there were pressures to end the service, and the hotly-disputed issue was put to a public vote. The result was to dispense with the tramway on the 30th September, but the decision was pre-empted by the facility itself, when the cable parted and the system literally came to a final halt. The breakage signalled the end of the last cable tramway to operate in England. Though its passing was predictable in the climate of the time, one can only speculate what a tourist feature the tramway would represent in this present age, bearing in mind the modern attractions available in nearby Matlock Bath, which operates its own aerial cableway.

TRAM DEPOT

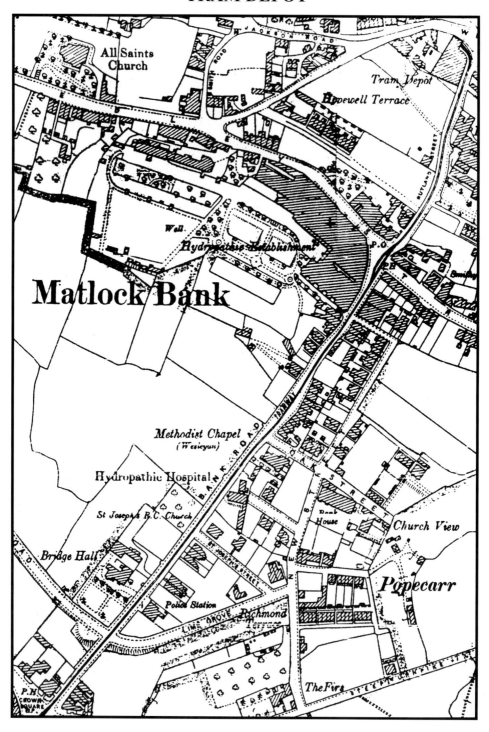

(left) 81. The cable tramway ran for over half a mile up the one-in-five/20% incline of Matlock Bank. The plan shows the layout, with turnouts in Crown Square (bottom left) and at Smedley Street. The tram shed was at the top of the hill (top right) alongside the offices and generating station.

82.   The driving force behind the cable tramline was Job Smith, who owned Malvern House Hydro on Smedley Street and was a councillor for Matlock UDC. This enabled him to apply pressure in favour of the project.

83.   George Croydon Marks was appointed engineer to the cable tram scheme. He had extensive experience in steep-gradient tramway work, and had designed and built the Lynton Cliff Railway.

84. The tram shed and offices are seen here under construction. Behind the workforce are the twin bay entrances for the cars. Note the fine wrought iron scrollwork below the door lintel, and the inquisitive lady viewing proceedings from the street at the top right.

85. The tram depot, which cost £2,600 to build, boasted a 100ft high chimney, plus offices and a waiting room. The double doors of the car shed can be seen behind the two gentlemen posed on the right.

TRACKLAYING

86.   Taken in Crown Square in 1892, looking uphill, this shot shows the terminal loop and the central rail slot for the tram gripper. Job Smith stands fourth on the left, in one of the fancy western-style hats he affected.

87.   Another view of the same scene, looking towards Matlock Bridge, reveals Job standing on the right behind the piled spoil. The dapper personage on the left in the bowler and sporting a gold watch chain, is obviously part of the management team.

88.   Further uphill, this scene pictures the rail being laid on the steepest part of the bank, on Rutland Street. The gritstone setts piled alongside the track were used as paving to cover all but the tramlines. Note the sharp curve to the line in the distance.

OPENING OF THE TRAMWAY

89.   All Matlock was *en fete* for the opening of the line, on 28th March 1893, as this Crown Square scene demonstrates. The floral arch bears the legend 'HERE SEEKING HEALTH AND PLEASURE, MAY ALL BOTH BLESSINGS FIND.' The tram below the arch has a uniformed band performing on the top deck, whilst George Newnes can be seen at bottom left, in front of the raised board. Toppers and bowler hats abound, and the square is tightly packed with celebrating locals.

90. A good shot of brand-new Car 3 on the Smedley Street loop at the inauguration of the service. Note the triangular dash panel, with the entrance step on the right of the tram. The omnipresent Job Smith appears halfway along the well-patronised upper deck, whilst the engineer, George C. Marks, can be seen on the extreme right, on the vehicle platform.

91. Job has shifted his position in this shot, presumably taken at the same time as picture 90. Smedley's Hydro, a vast edifice, now the Derbyshire County Council Offices, can be seen to the left, whilst the young gentleman below the rear stairs might well be Ernest 'Tram Fat' Smith, who later became the last manager of the facility. The intricate lining-out and company crest show up well on the waist panel, as do the bogie trucks and other salient features of the car.

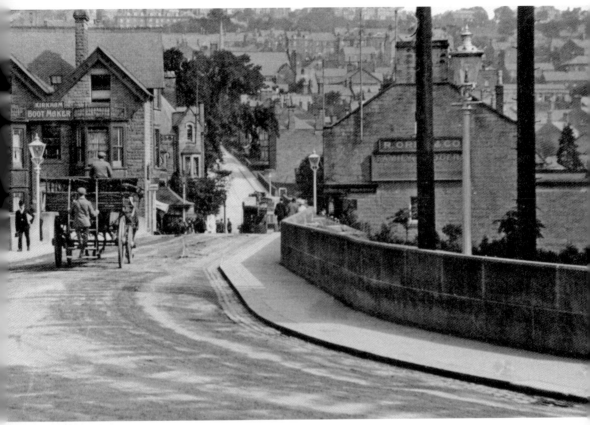

92.   The Crown square tram terminus as seen from Matlock Bridge, which spanned the Derwent, and which provided the approach into town from the railway station. Many summer visitors crossed the bridge to embark on the cars in order to ride up the bank. A service tram can be seen on the distant loop.

93.   A nostalgic view of one of the cars at the terminus. The ornate shelter to the left of the tram was built in 1899, though in this picture it has not yet received its elegant turreted clock. The shelter still survives in a nearby park, whilst the lettered glass panels are preserved at Crich Tramway Museum a few miles away.

94.   By the time this image was taken, the clock had been positioned on the shelter as a service car waits on the turnout. On the right a horse and trap awaits customers wishing to visit other parts of this pleasant dale.

95.　　Cable Car 3 is at rest on the loop, with the superb little shelter on the left and the Crown Hotel behind. Sadly the little edifice was swept away in 1927 as a traffic hazard – nowadays it might well have been scheduled or listed as a monument. Note the date, 1899, above the central doorway.

96.   This photograph reveals many interesting details as Car 2, bearing a board extolling 'ROCKSIDE HYDRO,' waits at the shelter. This hydro was at the top of the bank, and behind the tram shed. Note the 'TRAMS START HERE' notice above the horse's head on the left, and the individual hefting an advertising board on the right.

97.   Car 1 also bears a 'ROCKSIDE' board as it lingers alongside the superb and well-cared-for three-in-hand horse team pulling the charabanc on the left. In the distance a passenger-less Car 3 can be seen on the incline.

98.   Car 3 halts on the single stretch of line beyond the loop, with the bridge behind, and the rustic shelter on the right. In the early years the vehicles carried few if any advertisements.

99.   Another vista taken from the bank, showing Car 1. Rising behind the distant bridge is Masson Hill, which reaches an elevation of over 1100ft. The two fine horses on the right represent the alternative modes of transport available to the tourist, though none could tackle the steep Matlock Bank!

100. A post World War 1 shot picks out an imposing white-tyred touring car at bottom left, whose engine is receiving some attention, and a far-off tram on the gradient, whose steep slope has been somewhat flattened out by the camera. A 'CAR EVERY TEN MINUTES' sign has appeared on the shelter.

101.   Another post-war illustration reveals various automobiles in shot, and Car 3 loading for the uphill journey. Note also the new threat posed by the motorbus, whose bonnet can be seen behind the shelter on the left.

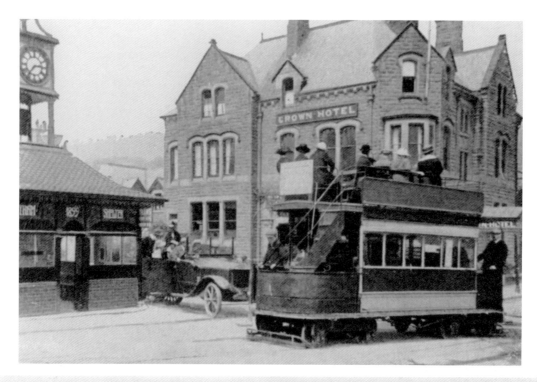

102.   Car 1, uncharacteristically bereft of adverts, stops by the shelter in this circa 1921 picture, whilst a well-loaded motor charabanc has replaced the earlier horse transport. Note how the ground actually slopes downwards on the right, before the ascent up the hill commences.

104.   Two trams pause in the square as the (literally) long arm of the law joins an inquisitive throng viewing work on the track. There was an underground chamber here, with a cable drum which needed regular greasing. On one occasion the greaser was forgotten, and remained trapped until someone released him by lifting the manhole cover. His comments were noted, but remain unprintable!

103.   The reason for the demise of the cable cars is clear in this view, as a Furniss motorbus on the left filches trade from the trams. Though these vehicles were incapable of climbing the steep hill, they touched on both termini via a roundabout route.

105.   Flooding was always a problem in the square, if heavy rains swelled the nearby Derwent. Here Car 1 negotiates the rising waters as it passes the hotel on the left. The driver is Bill Handley, accompanied by Routeman Will Swift.

BANK STREET

106.   A good view of the uphill climb from the bottom of Bank Street as Car 3 waits for the off, showing details of its upper deck floor and seating. On the down run drivers sometimes slacked off the gripper to give lady riders a thrill as the tram careered towards Crown Square, apparently out-of-control. However killjoys looking through the Town Hall windows at top left were sometimes suspected of reporting the errant car crews!

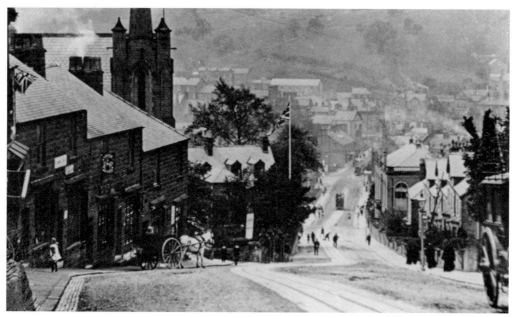

107.   This view, taken just above the Wesleyan Chapel on the left, shows not only the steepness of the slope , but the zig-zag bends on the line, all necessitating special pulleys to support the cable in its metal conduit. Note the two trams, one on the hill and another at the lower terminus.

108.   Just above the 110ft steeple of the chapel, Car 3 pauses on the ascent, with the driver either chatting or soliciting trade. The advertising boards on the left feature ENO'S FRUIT SALTS, LUX and Bakewell Show on 4th August, neatly dating the time of year. Again, Masson Hill looms behind the tram.

109.   Two vehicles pause side-by-side on the turnout with Smedley's Hydro behind. They appear in their new 1898 livery after the undertaking was gifted to the UDC whose title can be seen on the cant rail. The trams appear in pristine condition, with the only adverts carried on the dash panels. Note the smart uniforms of the crews, which include kepi-style caps.

110.   Cars 1 and 2, both sporting 'ROCKSIDE HYDRO' boarding, rest on the half-way loop. No.1 is presumably heading up Rutland Street to the top terminus by the tram depot. Bailey's on the left, was a well-known chemist, who also retailed ginger beer and mineral waters.

111. A worse-for-wear Car 2 parks in the same place as in the previous scene, with a loaded No.3 disembarking travellers before tackling the pull to Wellington Street and the bank-top hydros.

RUTLAND STREET

112.   Fully laden, Car 1 ascends the final stretch via the sharp curve on a fine sunny day. The tram is just above the Smedley Street turnout, with William Hand's garage visible just behind the tram.

113.   A distant cable car approaches the final, steepest part of the uphill run, with the tram buildings just in shot on the right at the top of Rutland Street. Note the fine scenic vista of Masson Hill on the opposite side of the valley. Tram travel here on such a day must have been a distinct pleasure.

CARS AND CREWS

114. Car 3, adverts confined to the dash panels, stairs and rocker panel, pauses for its picture by the wall outside the shed and offices. The crew appear in civvies, including a bowler-hatted driver, whilst the gentlemen on the right are presumably depot staff. The tarpaulin hanging behind the staircase must have offered protection against draughts

115. An excellent study of Car 1 includes the crew at the upper terminus. The driver, peering from under the stairs, was William Windley. On the right can be seen Car 3 at rest on the level area outside the shed. The window bill seems to indicate a fare rise.

116. The spartan interior of the cars can be appreciated in this picture, which shows the turtle-back roof, and the two-and-one arrangement of the slatted wooden seats with their swing backs. The saloon carried 13 inside places, with room for 18 more on the top deck.

LATTER DAYS

117. An end-of-service shot, pictures Car 2 waiting at the Crown Square terminus on a not too busy day. The 'ROCK CAFÉ' appears to be the 'in' place in 1927. Here the camera gives a good view of the uphill climb, with another far-off tram approaching the Smedley Street loop.

118. Three final 1927 images of Car 2 at Crown Square, all show excellent detail of the vehicles just before the closure. Here the tram, in obvious need of a good clean, picks up riders for the ascent, which is on the left.

119.   A windy day judging by the coat-tails of the passenger on the right, as the conductor of Car 2 passes behind the dash panel of the now empty tramcar. The little shelter is presumably hidden behind the vehicle.

120.   A final view of the cable car fleet, with No. 2's window bill promising a 'BIG NIGHT' with 'YOUNG APRIL', though exactly what kind of night is not specified! Note again the hanging tarpaulin and the decrepit state of the tram in its last few months of service.

MP Middleton Press

Easebourne Lane, Midhurst, West Sussex.
GU29 9AZ   Tel:01730 813169

www.middletonpress.co.uk   email:info@middletonpress.co.uk

EVOLVING THE ULTIMATE RAIL ENCYCLOPEDIA

A-0 906520   B-1 873793   C-1 901706   D-1 904474

OOP Out of Print at time of printing - Please check current availability   BROCHURE AVAILABLE SHOWING NEW TITLES